I0172963

LUMINOUS

LUMINOUS

Poems by
Ruby Hoy

PERILOUS SHORE PRESS
PORTSMOUTH, NH

2017

PERILOUS SHORE PRESS
249 Lincoln Avenue
Portsmouth, NH 03801-5148 USA

First Edition

Copyright 2017 by Ruby Hoy

All rights reserved, including
the right of reproduction in whole or in part in any form.

Book Design by Jeff Schwaner
Cover photograph by Joseph O'Connell

ISBN-13: 978-0692858608 (Perilous Shore Press)
ISBN-10: 0692858601

CONTENTS

THIS PERILOUS SHORE

BECOMING LUMINOUS

ABOUT THE AUTHOR

with gratitude for what we have

THE GAP BETWEEN STONE AND DREAMS

BELIEF

Seventeen degrees atop
the Shenandoah Mountain,
sun shines a day past
the Winter Solstice.
Surely, slowly,
we move to the light.
Spring is a promise
even the faithless
can believe in.

GREENLAND GAP

for my mother, Nelda Hanlin Hoy, who loved poetry

In Greenland Gap
West Virginia
the river flows fast and cold
tumbling over rocks
in its hurry to reach the falls,
then slides down
with a whoop and a holler
into a hole where trout
dream peaceably of other lives.
Along the way a jagged cliff
rears to one side
and on the other
a small sunlit meadow.
Only in the evening, just before sunset
do the rocks shine
having been all day
in darkness.

A WELL TRAVELED MAN

Jackie Daly tells a story about Paddy Killoughery, of
Doolin in County Clare, in the West of Ireland. Jackie
asked him if he had traveled much. He replied "I was
all over the place, up around our own place."

He knows every stone
in these green fields
and how they lay exposed
to the lashing rain, the summer sun,
where the sheep huddle
when the winter storms
fly in fury off the Atlantic,
the smell of the sea salt air
on a Sunday morning
when Spring first rises,
where hares leap and gambol,
and ravens call the twilight
home to roost.
He is well traveled
in the contours
of the heart's own country
and blessed by perceiving
one place well.

LIVING ON THE POLAR EQUATORIAL TRAIL

Having come at last
to a place of my own
I find that I am living
on the polar equatorial trail
settled in woods between
two rivers and a lake.
At night the sound
of trout dreaming
is followed by morning voices
of geese, and the cry
of the red-winged blackbird.
From my window I can see
hemlock, cedar, and pine,
the totems of my childhood.
I have planted a lilac bush,
thyme, rosemary, hollyhocks,
two kinds of mint.
My library of Petoskey stones
surrounds these borders
waiting patiently for the return
of the great inland seas,
when even rocks
may live again.

RENASCENT

From the rooftop in the soft
gloaming of a summer night
I see the past come ghosting
over the Bronx flowing out
from Van Cortland it covers
Norwood in hayfields shorn
of their second cutting.
A cow pokes her head
around the corner
of the Mexican grocery
lowing softly to her calf
at play in the spray
of the fire hydrant.
Up on Gun Hill the cries
of some few patriots dragging
a cannon to the top, firing down
on the British, still echo
through this veil of now.
Tibbet's Brook rises
from burial in the sewers,
remembers, as water may,
when the Algonquin named it
Mosholu, for smooth stones,
gleaming in the last gold light.
At the site of a small lake,
once called the Reservoir,
joggers circle the oval
and a drowned boy
wriggles through the fence,
bent on adventure never hearing
his mother's call to return.

SNOW MOON

The Snow Moon rises
over Portsmouth Harbor,
admires her reflection
in the waters past Kittery,
and tucking a stray cloud
behind her ear, sails
away to meet her lover
beyond the White Mountains.

RITUALS

A spring moon hangs
in the evening sky
a farmer burning brush
in the field
keeps an ancient ceremony
he does not name.
There is ritual in writing
in the placement of symbols on paper,
and in the slow movement
of my hands over your chest
the way a stream comes to know
the stones it has flowed
over for years.

COMING TO PENDLETON

Riding the hairpins
and switchbacks
off the Allegheny Mountain,
there above the gloaming's
last rose light
one star suspended
like hope
in a firmament of memory.

THE STONEMASON

for Jim Underwood

I saw a tundra swan
flying up river
over the South Branch
of the Potomac,
as though your spirit had
taken flight
winging its way
to whatever end awaits.
You once told me
you would return,
that in thirty years,
give or take,
there would be
a stonemason
ready to build the
house I imagined.
Perhaps time is not
linear and you
have already placed
each stone with
unerring precision
in a wall standing
on a farther shore,
where the sea lashes
the coast and mountains
rise to an azure sky
as flowers
blossom in the gap
between
stone and dreams.

DECEMBER SOLSTICE
PORTSMOUTH NH

I greet the solstice near the sea,
facing East as in burial,
though this is more of resurrection,
turning, as the natural year turns,
to the light that knows
no gravity but hope,
and in the end
is something more than grace.

BANISH DESPAIR

APRIL PORTSMOUTH NH

Crows are calling
the news of the morning
wake up wake up
daffodils are blooming

FIRST SUNDAY FOLLOWING THE FIRST FULL MOON AFTER THE VERNAL EQUINOX

We all have our rocks
to roll away
no sacrilege in saying so
no crime in new beginnings.
Roll away the real world
reel away the old world
dare to face East
and wait for the dawn.

ADVICE FROM THE MORRÍGAN

Trust
is the spear point
of courage
it opens the way
to joy.

Pain
comes in waves,
meet it
as the shore
meets the sea.

This life
comes but once,
live with your
whole heart,
love fiercely.

LIFE IS LIKE FISHING

Life is like fishing
you never know what you're going to get.
I've had my share of tiny perch
that nibble worms and refuse to be caught,
snagged many a lily pad,
lost good bass lures in the process.
I've caught turtles and lake grass
and nearly lost a finger trying
to remove a small pike from my line.
There were days when the bobber sat
unmoving on the still lake,
worms drowned in sacrifice
to the gods of patience and fair weather.
I've learned the sunny day is not the best
for fishing, and often good things come
beneath a cloudy sky.

THE COMMON HOURS

It is in the common hours
that we are most alone.
In the moment we turn
towards distant thunder
and firmly close a window,
or place one glass in the sink
switch off the lights
and move to a place
of dreaming.

THE DAPPLED GOAT

The black and white dappled goat
kneels beneath the black horse
at the edge of the empty pasture.

They may lead the unexamined life
with an uncertain future
but they do not lead it alone.

WISH AT MIDWINTER

Winter holds memory
like an icy jewel
flung against
a darkening sky.
Snowflakes shine
under the moon
a lost galaxy of stars
to wish upon.
I wish that we may
live gracefully
within the limits
of this life,
with a quiet mind,
a merry heart,
and love our amulet
against the seasons
of despair.

WHAT THE TITMOUSE TAUGHT ME

Don't be afraid.
Look for the good stuff.
Take what you find.
Fly away singing.

THE RED PAOLO SOPRANI

for John Redmond

The red Paolo Soprani
holds the jigs old men danced
in their wool jackets and battered caps
at the crossroads of memory.
It carries slow sad airs and marches,
a history that is talisman and burden.
Behind the buttons are barn dances
old women stepping in swirling skirts
when their hearts were light
and filled with hope.
Reels and hornpipes wait beside polkas
for his fingers to release them
and banish despair
from this century of doubt.

BLUE MOON

Summer surrenders
to autumn
in a blue moon
on the last day
of August.
Long ago
I surrendered
the things of no
consequence,
keeping only
the luminous bits,
shining, fragile
holding the dark
at bay.

CHASE THE RABBIT

GRINDINGLY EXCEEDINGLY FINE

When I was a girl Coyote looked
a great deal like my grandfather
and told me of a place
where trout gather to tell stories
of the times they got away.

My grandfather told stories
of how Coyote got away.

My daughters are upstairs pretending
to look for dead people
so they can take the shadows from them
and turn them into angels.
It could have been Coyote who gave them
this idea, it was not my grandfather.
 My friend is in jail for being
a drunken Indian,
something about an elevator,
a gumball machine, and a bottle
of sweet wine.

 My sense of humor is not what it was,
my grandfather is dead,
and I haven't seen Coyote
in a long, long time.

THE EPISTLE OF COYOTE: THE TRICKSTERS GUIDE TO THE UNIVERSE

1

we all
in the end
die
the trick
is that first
you must live

2

gratitude
is the key
to attitude
rejoice
in what
you have

3

understanding it
will not change
anything
a rock is a rock
a rabbit is a rabbit
chase
the rabbit

THE RETURN OF COYOTE

Coyote has recently returned
from a somewhat
extended sabbatical.
He has hung out his shingle,
an old wooden sign swaying
on a loop of rusty chain,
in Bronx Park.
You might say he's
come back to the 'hood
to raise a family but not
of course, to pay taxes.
The Trickster's services
are available to all
results guaranteed,
exactly what result is not
specified but you can
be sure of a result,
and follow him on Twitter.

BRER COYOTE

Me and Coyote are sitting on the shore of Lake Ontario, having a pithy philosophical discussion, or I am. He is pulling burrs out of the base of his tale with his teeth, one leg cocked jauntily over his shoulder. "Gravity and Time take a terrible toll," I muse. "True," he says. "Humans, mountains, even these shining waters, all wear down, and just when you figure it out, poof, you're dust." "Right," I say. "Do you think that damned rabbit has gotten out of the briar patch by now?" he asks as he lopes toward a patch of blackberries. I smile fondly at this flea bitten, disreputable, piece of God. The Trickster always lives in the moment.

THIS PERILOUS SHORE

GATHERED TO THE RIVER

It is raining in Michigan
rivers retrieve their losses
as trees ache into bloom.
We sat on the concrete bridge
above the Chippewa River,
our blessings already spent
in whiskey and water,
currents too strong to fight.
A river runs south through Ohio
with no knowledge of its loss,
water forgets the steps
of saint or sinner and buries
its ghosts with no names.
Today I live in the north
with losses I cannot bear,
gathering them to the banks
of this perilous shore.

BLACKBIRD

A red-winged blackbird cries
to his mate in the middle of March
along the edge of a frozen lake.
Oh, to have such simple faith.

HOLDING SACRED

Days shorten to the solstice,
and we live as we are willing
lives lost before us,
as winter snow covers only what we see,
and we see so little.
We have yielded to this life
a part of us which does not
long for comfort or warmth,
that belongs in the cleansing cold
checking trap lines, reading signs
in the snow and the sky,
and what have we kept?
What shall we hold sacred
through these long winters of the blood?
Tonight I hold only bourbon
and walk alone as the Great Bear
tilts crazily overhead.
I curse comfort, warmth, and whiskey
and feel the past move too clearly
along the fine ridges of my bones.

LANDSCAPE OF THE HEART

An early snow
on the rolling
glacial ridges
of Antrim County,
bare trees stand
like sentinels,
crimson sumac
blazes bright
in the foreground,
this landscape
of the heart
held ever
in my memory.

NO SUNDAY SALES

The trees in McIntosh's orchard
stand stalwart
against the skies of December,
face snow and ice with serenity,
certain of their place, graced
with promises to keep,
Cortland, Transparent, Delicious,
Jonathon, Rome, and Spy,
a litany of apples.
For three generations
these trees have held their ground
asking only work
and reverence.

REPLY TO JAMES WRIGHT FROM A BACK ROAD IN GLADWIN COUNTY MICHIGAN

Many summers I have lived here
traveling Michigan's green leafy tunnels,
dust flying behind the car
we rush down washboard roads,
and somehow I've grown here
become a woman who does not believe in answers
expecting nothing to come easy.

Today I take my daughters
driving down these country roads,
their laughter rises from the back seat
floats out over bracken and Juneberry bushes
and settles with the dust.
It no longer matters
if I have wasted my life.

LIVING IN MICHIGAN

for Marc Sheehan who wonders why he still lives in Michigan

Have you really forgotten why?
Forgotten the feel of a sun
warmed concrete dam
over the Chippewa river,
how the water is the color
of bourbon, and how our dreams
took flight before our lives
became anchors?
Forgotten the rapids on the Grand
that named a city,
the feel of snow on your face
like a lover's kiss?
Forgotten salmon fighting
their way over the weir
at Charlevoix?
Forgotten the pull of Superior,
a cosmic lodestone of such power,
that it seems a privilege
to drown there.
Forgotten the long blue line
of summer on Lake Michigan,
sunrise over Huron,
the Straits of Mackinaw,
and the endless inland lakes
full of perch and bluegill,
bullfrogs and cattails.
In winter you can even walk
on the water.

THE PLANTING

for John Dague

These high hills and ridges
of northern Michigan
may be no more
than glacial afterthought,
but as the spring comes
he will go into these fields
and mark them
with the precise geometry
of a farmer's love.

GLACIAL MEMORY

I want to live again
where spring is sung into being
by red-winged blackbirds,
where the echo of Lake Iroquois
shadows the shoreline
and the shining water remembers
the scent of the sea
and the fires of the First Nations.
Where summer's long twilight stretches to the horizon
and nearly makes up
for the dark dreary winter when the lakes
grow so cold that Coho and Lake Trout
come near the shore to be caught,
and you can almost hear
the slow sliding sound of glaciers.

TAKING THE BAIT

Sure and we have missed our calling,
all those years in academe,
the jobs for universities, non-profits, even industry,
and the good ones - house painting,
and Christmas tree sales,
none of these were where we belonged.
It seems so clear in hindsight,
a shack by the river, or lake in the U P
a big tub for minnows, and
a nice collection of worms,
night crawlers, red worms, the usual suspects.
A few Zebco reels and poles on the wall,
some bobbers, line, hooks, nets,
jitterbugs, spinners and spoons,
canvas creels and rubber waders.
The good life could have been ours.

BECOMING LUMINOUS

CREDO

I believe
in the power
of the minor keys,
in love unrepentant,
and desire,
honed and polished
to a fine
dark brilliance.

WOLF MOON

The full moon
makes me itch,
my lips
my tongue
and the back
of my throat,
between my legs,
and all over
my breasts.
Baby
I want you
to scratch it.

LITANY

Grant me the grace
to love fearlessly,
without condition
without expectation
without reservation,
let me love
like a waterfall tumbling
to a deep quiet pool,
like the light
of a harvest moon,
like the promise
of spring beneath
the snows of winter.

IF WISHES WERE HORSES

if wishes were horses time would
stop and in that sacred place
where fear dies you might know
all the seasons of my heart

an April evening as the chorus
of spring peepers sings the mountain
to sleep and the western sky
clings to a last thread of crimson

the smell of the forest when the sun's
first warmth wakens the ground
and mushrooms rise like a stand
of phalluses under the trees

June nights on the porch swing
a whippoorwill calling sadly
on a far hill in the gloaming
the magic of the first fireflies

the long languid summer days
without end or retribution
when Orioles nest in the catalpa
and cicadas call from the trees

two hawks flying in autumn
over fiery branches of maple and oak
to a high rock ledge gleaming gold
in the last blessing of twilight

a crisp cold October morn
when leaves crackle beneath your feet,
and time is lost in wood smoke
and memory is the amulet of despair

the first snow on the meadow
falling softly as the dream of faerie,
covering the land in promise
and a diamond dust of hope

a winter solstice so clear and
bright that stars could be caught
and held in our hands and we wake
to a season turned to light

BLACKBIRDS FLY

Holding her face
in his hands
he kissed her
and every scar
her spirit bore
lifted and flew away
like blackbirds
at first light.

SMALL MIRACLES

and still I dream
of making love
to you under the stars
the smell of wood smoke
and pine needles
and only an owl
to hear me scream
your name to the god
of small miracles

NAMES OF THE DECEMBER MOON

As the Long Nights Moon climbs
past snow over Afton Mountain
to hang argent in the December sky,
I would wrap my legs around you
pull you deep inside my warmth,
while the Cold Moon, the Snow Moon,
the last full moon of the year,
smiles down on us as we
become luminous.

TOTEMS

These are my totems:
a wren singing in slanted light
after the autumnal equinox,
crows calling in winter,
a Labrador Retriever in any season,
wolves, red tailed hawks,
cedar, white pine,
the roar of Lake Superior
breaking on Whitefish Point,
the smell of the sea on the coast of Clare,
and the sound of your breathing
as you sleep beside me.

THE GRACE OF GOD

loving you is
sacrament
you are that
piece of God
reflected
in my life
compass for
the journey
and anchor
to my heart

LETTING IN THE LIGHT

In the dark
of a winter's night
let the empty places
inside you crack
and shatter like shards
of ice on tree branches,
falling away
in glittering pieces that
melt in the morning sun.
The light comes in where
we are broken.

LAST CALL

we do not
see the song
of our lives
between
the ending
and now
but when the wheel
of the world
stops spinning
and peace settles soft
and dark
as a raven's wing
let the melody
of your hands
be my last
memory

ACKNOWLEDGMENTS

Thank you to the publications where some of these poems, or different versions of them, previously appeared: Coyotes Journal, Green River Review, Hiram Poetry Review, Hudson View, Red Cedar Review, and Split Rock Review; and to the Irish Books Arts and Media Conference for selecting "Belief" as winner of their poetry contest.

ABOUT THE AUTHOR

Ruby Hoy has published in Red Cedar Review, Hiram Poetry Review, Coyote's Journal, and Split Rock Review, among others. She won poetry prizes from the Milwaukee Irish Festival, Irish Books Arts and Music Conference, and was a finalist for the Richard Snyder Memorial Publication Prize. Born in the north woods of Michigan, now living in New Hampshire, she works in the world of Irish traditional music, and does not spend enough time fishing.

www.ingramcontent.com/pod-product-compliance
Lightning Source LLC
Chambersburg PA
CBHW032053040426
42449CB00007B/1101